SECRET CODES AND HIDDEN MESSAGES

Jeffrey A. O'Hare

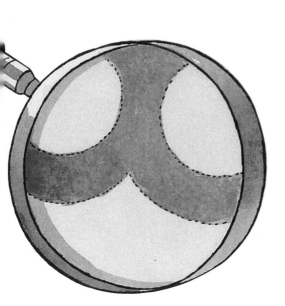

Boyds Mills Press

CONTRIBUTORS:

Shirley Marshall

Donna Rehm Siple

Jeanette Grote

Joe Seidita

Karen Morrell

Donna Lugg Pape

Don DiMarco

Diane Cherkerzian

Mark Malcolm

Isobel Livingstone

Copyright © 1997 by Boyds Mills Press
All rights reserved

Published by Bell Books
Boyds Mills Press, Inc.
A Highlights Company
815 Church Street
Honesdale, Pennsylvania 18431
Printed in the United States of America

This material was previously published in the Highlights for Children series PUZZLEMANIA.
Publisher Cataloging-in-Publication Data
O'Hare, Jeffrey A.
   Secret codes and hidden messages / by Jeffrey A. O'Hare.—1st ed.
[48]p. : col. ill. ; cm.
Summary : Dozens of codes and hidden messages are presented as riddles, poems and other fun-filled expressions.
ISBN 1-56397-652-8
1. Ciphers—Juvenile literature. 2. Riddles—Juvenile literature. 3. Picture puzzles—Juvenile literature. [1. Ciphers. 2. Riddles. 3. Picture puzzles.]
I. Title.
793.73—dc20   1997   CIP
Library of Congress Catalog Card Number 96-86534

First edition, 1997

10 9 8 7 6 5 4 3 2

SECRET CODES
AND
HIDDEN MESSAGES

TABLE OF CONTENTS

INTRODUCTION

SVOOL! DVOXLNV GL HVXIVG XLWVH ZMW SRWWVM NVHHZTVH.

Huh? What foreign language is that?

Actually, the language is English. But the message is hidden in a secret code.

This code is one of the best known because of its simplicity. It uses a reverse alphabet as shown here:

A=Z B=Y C=X D=W E=V F=U

G=T H=S I=R J=Q K=P L=O M=N

Whenever you see a **Z** in this particular code, it stands for the letter **A**. And the reverse means that an **A** stands for the letter **Z**.

A code is really just a specialized language, where the key is shared among a select group of people. Sometimes only you and a friend will have the key to a certain code. Other codes will be known to a larger group of people.

Codes are used for a variety of reasons. Sometimes they are used for secret communications. But very often a code will actually make it easier to get an idea across. For example, **CD-Rom** is the accepted code for **Compact Disc - Read Only Memory**. The shortened code form is much easier to say.

You may not know it, but you are already familiar with many code signs and symbols.

For instance, take these road signs:

Each sign here is a code that has a distinct meaning. You probably already know that the first sign means there are railroad tracks ahead. The second sign means the road is about to curve. The last sign tells drivers there is a school crossing ahead, and that they should watch out for children crossing the street. Whew! That would be a lot of information to fit on one sign. Luckily, there's a code symbol that means the same thing.

Codes are not always written. Sometimes a code can be spoken. During World War II, members of the Navajo tribe were code talkers for the United States. The Navajo language is so complex that only the tribe members could speak it, and no one could break its "code."

Some codes are everyday languages. People with disabilities sometimes can't understand or use the same language as other people, so specialized languages are developed. For example, Braille is used by the blind and visually impaired and Sign is used by the hearing impaired. These functional or "coded" languages make it much easier to communicate and understand.

Other examples of common codes found around the world include Morse Code (a series of dots and dashes used by telegraph operators), Semaphore (which uses different flag positions to send messages over a distance), and Heiroglyphics (picture messages left by ancient Egyptians).

Working through this book will help you understand how codes work. Once you know how a picture or a symbol can stand for a letter or word, you can develop your own codes. Use anything you like—numbers, letters, pictures, or other words. Or you can combine all these things into one code.

The code wheel on pages 16-17 is one way to make a code that changes every time you send a message. You'll need to give your partner a clue so he or she knows where to set the wheels to decode your message. A good clue might be to start your message with a note, such as **A=G**. That way the receiver knows to set the code wheel so that the **A** in the outer wheel is above the **G** in the inner wheel. Then the message should be easy to decode.

A wide variety of codes is featured in this book. You'll get a feel for a lot of different code forms, so you can choose the ways you like best to send a coded message. You'll also uncover a lot of fun poems, riddles, and other messages along the way.

Don't let the symbols in any message make you nervous. Once you get an idea of its key, you'll be able to crack almost any code.

There are a few things you can do to get better at working with coded messages. Do a lot of word puzzles, like word searches or crosswords. As you become more familiar with the shape and structure of words, codes will be easier to break.

Look for simple substitutions. Sometimes a code is very basic. A picture of a house may simply mean "house." Try the easy things first and then look for the more complicated.

Here's another easy subsitution code:

8-15-23 4-9-4 20-8-5 19-16-25 7-5-20 19-9-3-11?
8-5 8-1-4 1 3-15-4-5 9-14 20-8-5 14-15-19-5!

Each number here stands for one letter in the alphabet. In this case, A=1. That clue should help you get started.

7-15-15-4 12-21-3-11!

The Best Hidden Message Is an Invisible One

Perhaps you'd like to send a hidden message to a friend, but don't want anyone to know that a message has been sent. One way to send such a hidden message is to use invisible ink. To be especially tricky, write your message in code.

1. To make your own invisible ink, get some lemon juice or apple juice. If you don't have premade juice, you can use the juice right from the fruit itself.

2. Use a small stick, like a toothpick or a cotton swab, to write your message on a piece of paper. Put the stick into the juice first to wet it. (Be careful. If the stick is too dry, the "ink" won't show up. If it's too wet, the paper will get sloppy).

3. Once the stick is wet, write with it as if it were a pen. It may look as if nothng is happening, but the juice is leaving a trail on the paper that can be revealed later. You will probably need to wet your stick a few more times to complete your entire message.

4. You can even put your message on a piece of paper, let it dry, and then write a regular message over it with pen or pencil. That way no one will ever suspect there's another secret message hidden underneath.

5. When your friend wants to read your secret message, he or she must hold the note up in front of or over a light bulb. The light showing through the paper will reveal the juice message. The heat from the bulb helps to "cook" or age the juice to make it appear. Be careful not to let the bulb burn the paper.

FUN FINGERS

This code features the manual or hand alphabet used primarily by deaf people to fingerspell words. See if you can use the alphabet below to decode the limerick on the next page.

A B C D E F

G H I J K

L M N O P

Q R S T U

V W X Y Z

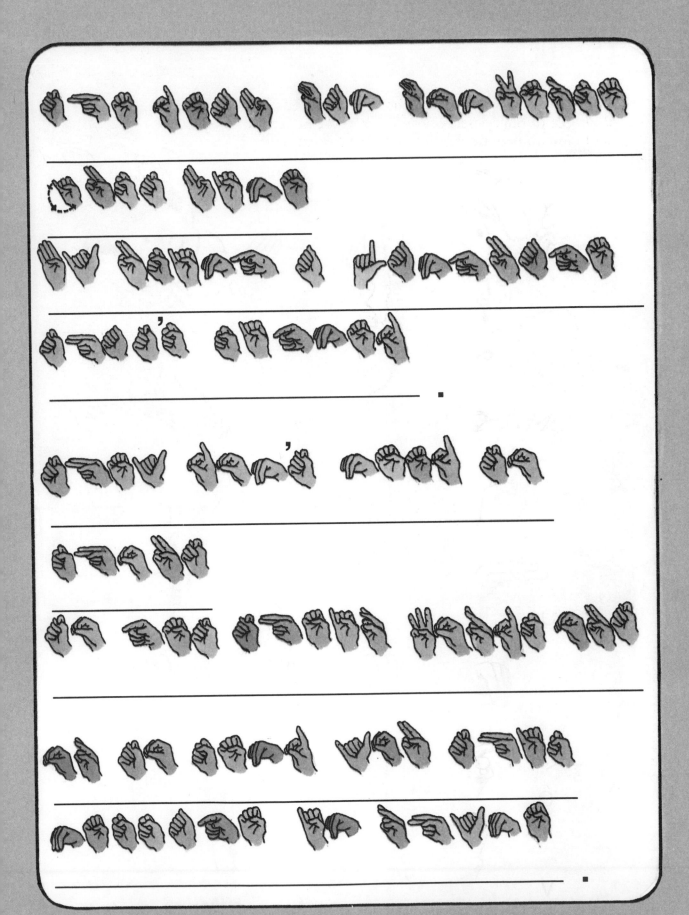

DOTS ALL

Beatrice learned a new code at her Scout meeting. The letters are made up of dots and dashes and are all called Morse code. To discover what she wrote using this new code, decipher the letters on the next page. A single slash represents spaces between letters, while a double slash separates the words.

A . —	N — .
B — . . .	O — — —
C — . — .	P . — — .
D — . .	Q — — . —
E .	R . — .
F . . — .	S . . .
G — — .	T —
H	U . . —
I . .	V . . . —
J . — — —	W . — —
K — . —	X — . . —
L . — . .	Y — . — —
M — —	Z — — . .

comma — — . . — —
period . — . — . —
question mark . . — — . .

._ _ / . . . . / ._ / _ // ._ / ._ . / . //

_____

_ / . . . . / . // _ / . . . . / ._ .. / . / . //

_____

_ _ ._ / . ._ / . . / _ ._ . / _ ._ . / . / . . . / _ //

_____

._ _ / ._ / _ ._ _ / . . . // _ _ _ / . . _ . //

_____

. . . / ._ _ ._ / ._ . / . / ._ / _ . . / . . / _ . / _ _ . //

_____

._ // . . . / . / _ . ._ ./ . _ . / . / . / _ // .._ _ ..

_____

_ / . / . ._ .. / . / . / _ _ . / . . . / _ _ _ / _ . / . / _ _ .. _ _ //

_____

_ / . / . ._ .. / . / . / _ _ . / . . . / ._ . / . ._ . / ._ _ . / . . . . / _ _ .. _ _ //

_____

._ / _ . / _ . . // _ / . / . / _ . . / . ._ .. //

_____

_ ._ _ / _ _ _ / . . _ / ._ _ . // ._ . . / . . / _ / _ / ._ _ . . / . //

_____

. . . / . . . / . . . / _ / . / ._ _ . / . ._ _ ._ _ ._

_____

Answers on page 48

FLAG FUN

Semaphore is a method of sending messages over great distances by using flags. It was once popular on ships and with the Boy Scouts. Use the semaphore alphabet shown below to decode the message on the next page.

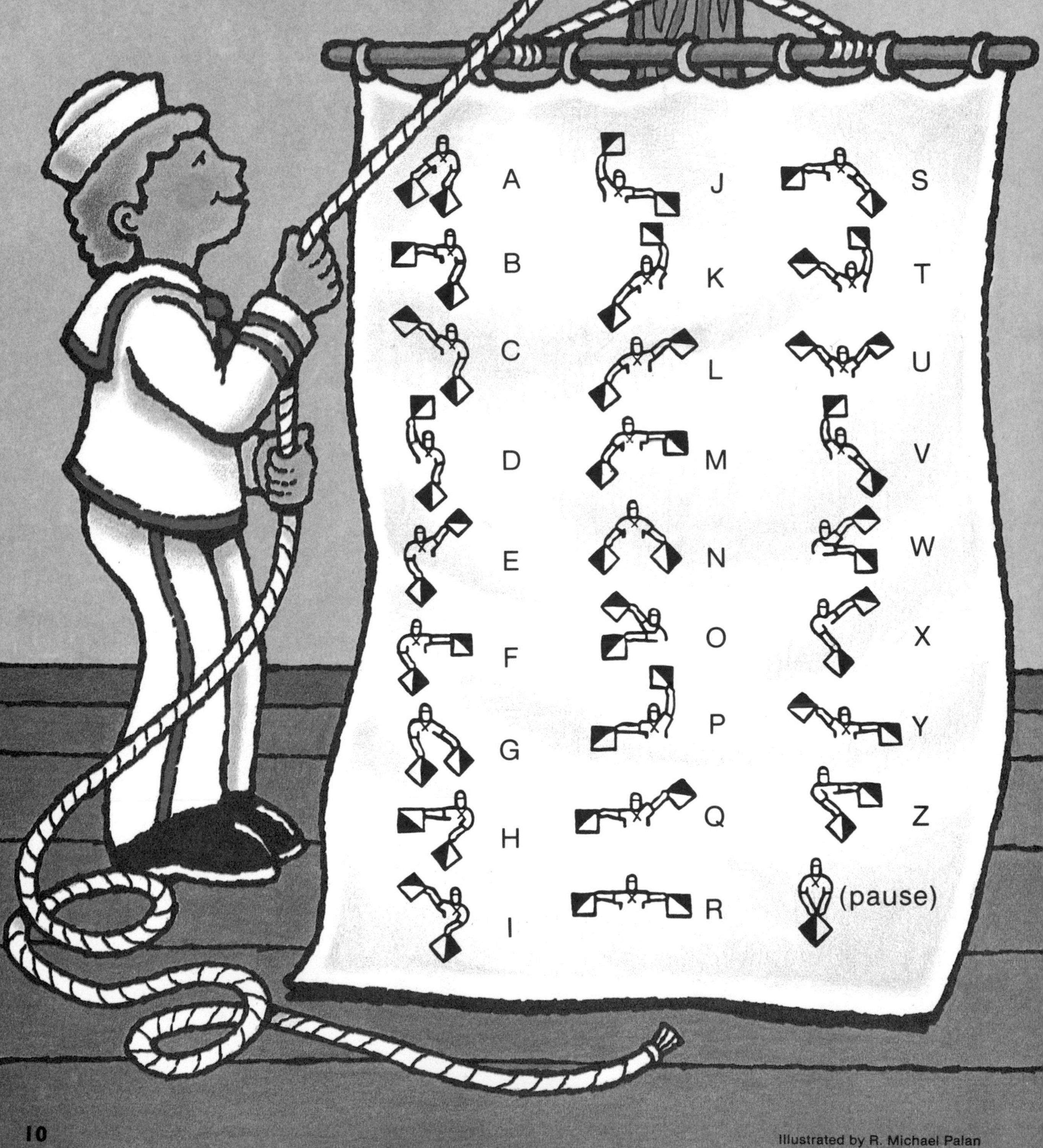

A   J   S
B   K   T
C   L   U
D   M   V
E   N   W
F   O   X
G   P   Y
H   Q   Z
I   R   (pause)

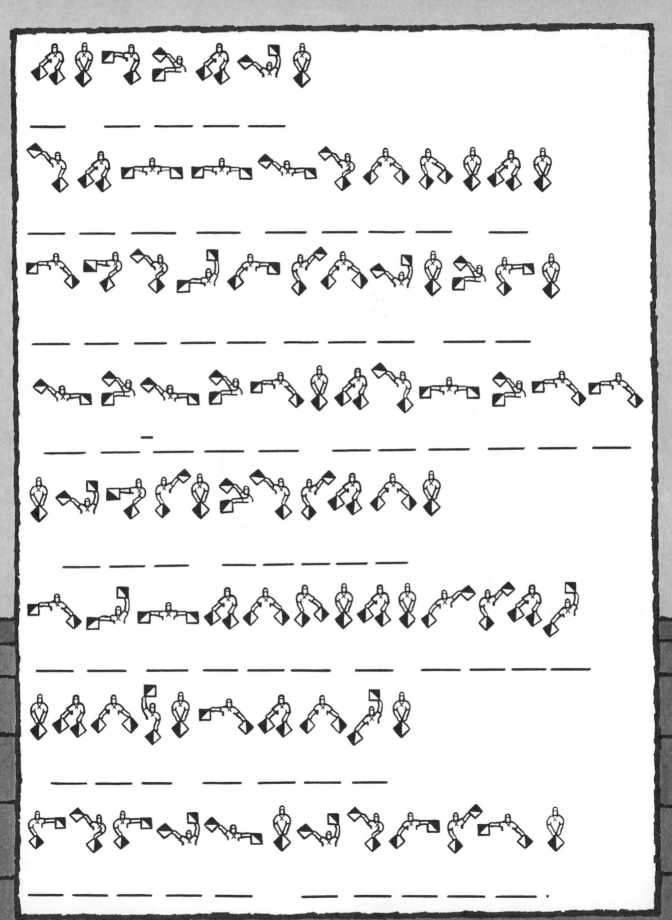

Answers on page 48

A TOUCHY LANGUAGE

These may look like a simple set of dominoes, but they are actually much more. These dots are a language that millions of people use everyday. Use the key below to translate the message and find out what this language is all about.

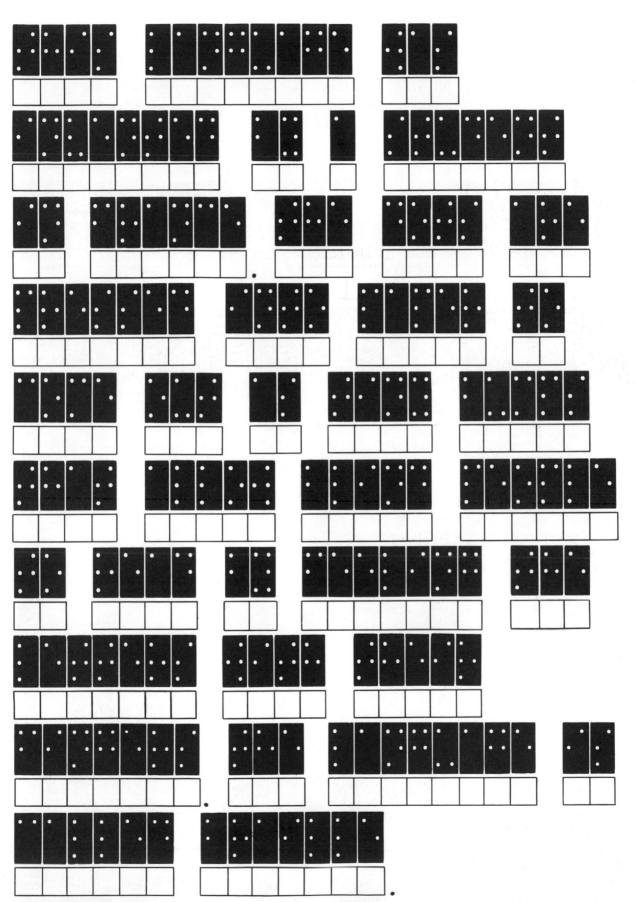

BOAT CODE

The names of some famous ships are flying in these flags. Use the code below to decipher the name of each. These flags show a real code that is used by boats and ships to send messages.

Illustrated by John Nez

TRAFFIC STOPPERS

The members of the Code Crackers Club are holding a big money-raising car wash. Of course, their signs are in code. They hope motorists will be curious enough to stop. Can you read their signs? The coded letters (in red) are on the outside of the code wheel. The letters you need to crack this code are on the inside.

Code Wheel

Answers on page 48

Illustrated by John Bennett

GOAT TELL YOUR MOTHER

There are plenty of fruits and vegetables to be picked in this farmyard. Use the clues to gather the letters that will give you the answer to the first goat's question. The clue numbers tell you where to put the right letters in the spaces. The first letter has already been picked to get you started.

1 - The first letter is on the tree that George Washington is believed to have chopped down.

2 - Now pick the letter from the vines that some say belong to a vegetable and some say belong to a fruit.

3 - This letter is attached to a long vegetable that rabbits like.

4 - This letter is on the fruit tree that sounds like there are two things together.

5 - After you pick the letter from this red fruit tree, you shouldn't have to go to the doctor today.

6 - Stalk the vegetables that are all ears and you'll find letter number six.

7 - Halloween is the best time to get the letter from these big vegetables.

8 - The eighth letter is in the vineyard, attached to fruits that are good for jelly, jam and juice.

9 - There is a fruit that shares its name with its color. That's where you can get the next letter.

10 - The yellow covering on this fruit can't be eaten, but they make good slippers.

11 - The next letter is hiding among the leaves near the heads of these leafy green vegetables.

12 - This vegetable only has eyes for you.

Illustrated by Lynn Adams

ROUNDABOUT RIDDLE

Why is your nose in the middle of your face? To find the answer, carefully follow the directions from square to square on this page and the next. Pick up a letter in each square, and write it in the next space below until the answer is complete. The first one is already filled in.

Answer: <u>B</u> __ __ __ __ __   __ __ , __

"__ __ __   __ __ __ __ __ __ __ ."

START Go two squares east and one square south. B	Go down four squares and right six squares. V	Go south two squares, then east two squares. O	Go to the bottom square of this column. E
Go to the third square from the bottom in the next column to the right. T	Go five squares to the right. H	Go to the green square in the last column on the next page. E	Go south two squares. A
Go to the fourth square from the bottom in the first column on the next page. W	Go to the first square in the first column of the second page. E	Go east four squares. R	Go down one square and up three. L
Go two squares north and five squares east. E	Go east two squares, then north four squares. P	Go six squares to the right of this one. U	Go three squares to the right. N

FINISH R	Go east three squares then left two squares. M	Go to the bottom corner square of the left page. D	Go to the square below the "start" square. S	Go south one square and west five squares. C
Go three squares south and two squares west. A	Go up one square and left five squares. R	Go south three squares. U	Go west four squares and north two squares. Y	Go down four squares. D
Go to the second square from the bottom in the last column. M	Go to the red square in this column. I	Go to the blue square at the bottom of this page. E	Go north one square and west one square. N	Go to the left four squares and up one square. C
Go south one square and north four squares. F	Go two squares east and three squares north. T	Go four squares to the right. Z	Go north two squares and west five squares. K	Go up three squares. G
Go four squares northeast. S	Go to the square to the right of the "start" square. H	Go to the orange square in the second column on the first page. T	Go to the bottom square in the first column on the previous page. J	Go to the bottom square in the first column in the previous page. S

THE ROYAL FAMILY

Fester the Jester played a trick on the royal family. All their name tags are in a secret code. Help King Kesworth crack the code on the tags, so the family can get on with their party. Hints: The code letters are the same for every tag. Each person has his or her royal title on a name tag.

GEOOR PHORQIFAR

VURP VOLHIZNT

XZURJO HMFFA

FIZQ FMZZA

XZURJOLL XOMZF

KMZIR KMZZMJEQM

QEJTOLL NOZOLM

JIERNOLL LMZMT

Illustrated by Lynn Adams

Answers on page 48

DOTS A LOT

The answer to the riddle is hidden in the graph. Start in the first vertical column. Go from top to bottom, copying any letters where you find a dot into the blanks at the bottom. Do the same thing with all columns until the blanks are filled in and the answer is revealed.

Answers on page 48

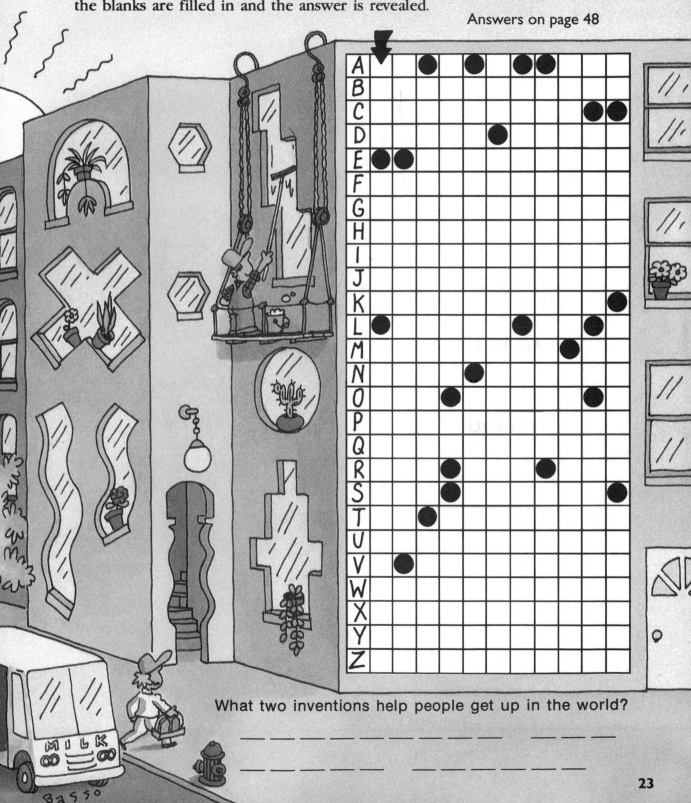

What two inventions help people get up in the world?

_ _ _ _ _ _ _ _ _ _

_ _ _ _ _ _ _ _

A CRYPTIC CRYPT

To find the answers to some really old jokes, use the hieroglyphics below to crack this crypt's code.

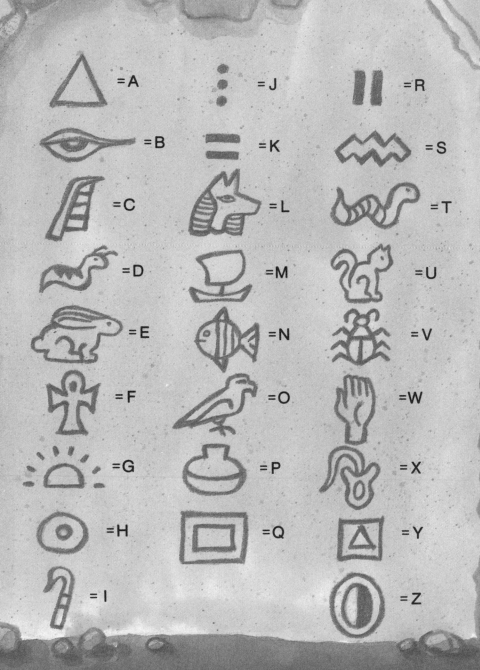

= A   = J   = R

= B   = K   = S

= C   = L   = T

= D   = M   = U

= E   = N   = V

= F   = O   = W

= G   = P   = X

= H   = Q   = Y

= I   = Z

Why couldn't the mummy go to the Monster Mash party?

How does a mummy get help in a good hotel?

Illustration by Richard Johnson

A CLEAN CODE

The letters of each word in these riddles are plotted on this graph.
Above each space are two numbers. The first number represents
the row, and the second is for which column in that row to stop
at. For example, 42 means row 4, column 2, which is an H. Can
you figure out the other letters in these riddles?

```
      1  2  3  4  5  6
  1   H  P  U  L  E  O
  2   B  I  A  D  H  Y
  3   E  U  T  O  S  G
  4   W  H  O  I  R  T
  5   Y  L  R  A  N  H
  6   A  S  G  D  C  W
```

1. 66 25 54 33   64 16   51 34 13   65 23 52 14

— — — —   — —   — — —   — — — —

22 46   66 42 15 55   12 44 63 35   24 43

— —   — — — —   — — — —   — —

33 56 31 22 45   52 61 32 55 64 53 26

— — — — —   — — — — — — — —?

11 43 36 41 54 62 25

— — — — — — — .

2. 41 56 15 45 31   24 43   62 25 15 31 12

— — — — —   — —   — — — — —

63 31 46   33 42 15 22 53   25 54 44 53   65 13 46

— — —   — — — — —   — — — —   — — —?

54 33   46 42 31   21 23 54   21 61 23   62 11 34 12

— —   — — —   — — —   — — —   — — — .

ICE-CREAM CODES

At Ira's Ice-Cream Igloo, they're always trying new riddles on their customers. Anyone who can figure out Ira's message gets free sprinkles on his or her ice cream. See if you can use the menu below to decipher Ira's latest riddle.

Illustrated by R. Michael Palan

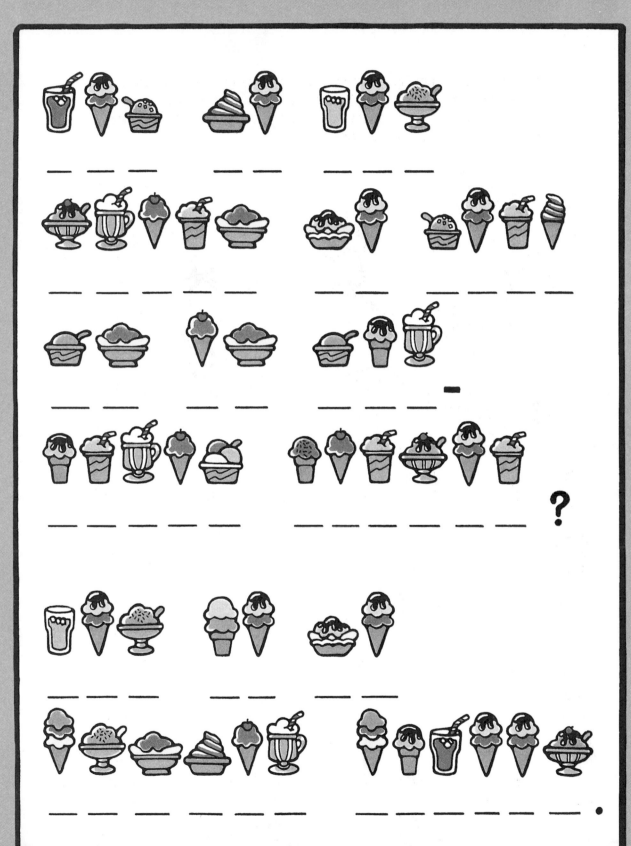

MUSICAL MERRIMENT

At the end of band practice, Erin used her music papers to leave a secret joke for her friend, Kerry. Using the code, see if you can play out Erin's message.

Illustrated by Anni Matsick

Answers on page 48

THE MYSTERY OF THE CASTLE

Eric and his parents visited a castle in England one summer. Before he went inside, Eric noticed a pattern of unusual markings on the many stones that formed the front wall of the castle. Each marking was made up of two or more connecting lines and one dot. Eric believed that the markings contained a secret message, but he could not figure out how to read it. Later, inside the great hall of the castle, Eric saw something carved in the stone on one of the walls.

● ● ●	● ● ●	● ● ●
A B C	D E F	G H I
● ● ●	● ● ●	● ● ●
J K L	M N O	P Q R
● ● ●	● ● ●	● ●
S T U	V W X	Y Z

Suddenly, Eric understood how to read the message on the front of the castle. He ran outside to see what it said. Can you read the secret message?

Starter Hint: = MY

32

Illustrated by John Nez

TAKE THE FIELD

To answer the question below, you've got to play ball.
Follow the directions to get the letters and then place them in
their positions. All spaces marked with the same number get the
same letter. Now step up to the plate and take your best shot!

Why is it farther from second base to third
than it is from first base to second?

| 1 | 2 | 3 | 4 | 5 | 6 | 2 | | 7 | 8 | 2 | 9 | 2 | 6 |,

| 4 | | 6 | 8 | 10 | 9 | 7 | 6 | 7 | 10 | 11 |

| 12 | 13 | | 1 | 2 | 7 | 14 | 2 | 2 | 13 |.

VISIT
H
S
E

HOT
DOGS →

191

Illustrated by R. Michael Palan

34

The pitcher is about to throw letter number one.

Letter number six is flashing on the scoreboard.

Pick up the eleventh letter at first base, the ninth letter at second, and the third letter at third.

Letter number twelve is on home plate.

The fourth letter is on the catcher's back.

You can find the eighth letter in the bleachers and the fourteenth letter on the mascot's shoulder.

The blimp is carrying the fifth letter.

The center fielder is in front of letter number thirteen.

Look in the dugout for the second letter.

The seventh letter is on the batter's helmet.

Letter ten is about to be caught in right field.

RIDING THE RAILS

Ride the Cannonball Express and help pick up every mailbag. At each stop, write the code number of the mailbag in the boxes across the middle row of the answer. The first two are done to get you on the right track. At the end of your run, use the chart to figure out what code letter was in each mailbag. The message will spell out the answer to the station master's question.

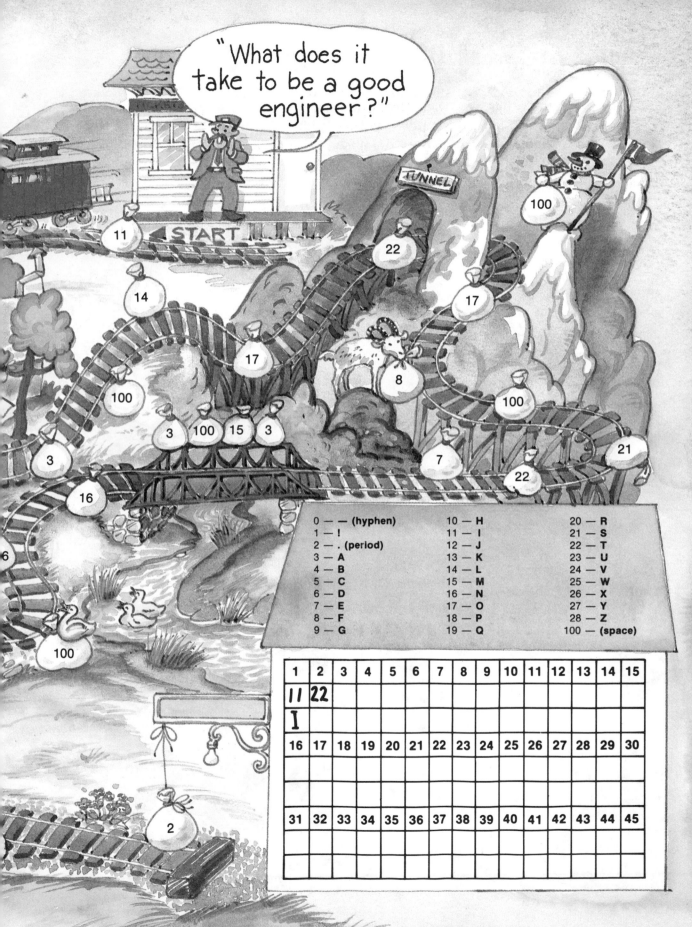

LOOK OUT BELOW!

Can you answer the crab's question? Follow the directions to find the letters you need. Put each letter in the right spaces, placing the same letters on spaces with similar numbers. When you're done, you will find the answer, as well as the location of the missing baby.

$$\overline{}\ \overline{}\ \overline{}\ \overline{}\ \overline{}\ \overline{}\ \overline{}\ \overline{}\ \overline{}\ \overline{}\ \overline{}\ \overline{}$$

1 2 3 4 5 6 7 8 8 9 10 1

"Who snatched the baby octopus and held it for ransom?"

Dive way down below the kelp to find letter number 7.

In the treasure chest lies the third letter.

The ninth letter is hanging from the sea horse's tail.

Explore the sunken wreck. The second letter is in the porthole. The eighth letter is on the steering wheel.

The clam is holding the fifth letter, while the shark has the tenth letter.

The crab's letter is a phony, but the starfish has the real sixth letter.

The fourth letter is sticking out of the sand.

Watch out for the ray who has a false letter.

You can find letter number one in the ship's crow's nest, along with the sleeping baby.

Answers on page 48

Illustrated by Lynn Adams

CORNY CODE

Pick the letters off the pictured objects
to solve two fun riddles.

What kind of fruit do scarecrows like?

Why are cornstalks good listeners?

Answers on page 48

HARD TIMES

It's time for a new code. First, look at the times beneath each space in the code. Next, find the matching times on one of the clocks. Fill in the code spaces with the letters shown on the matching clocks to reveal two riddles and their answers. Work quickly before time runs out.

1.

___ ___ ___ ___ ___ ___ ___ ___ ___
8:15 3:45 6:15 6:23 2:15 6:23 3:05 3:45 3:10

___ ___ ___ ___ ___ ___ ___ ___ ___
5:23 4:05 7:55 5:23 10:26 6:00 3:10 3:05 12:30

___ ___ ___ ___ **?**
2:55 12:30 9:25 3:45

___ ___ ___ ___ ___ ___ ___ ___
2:15 3:05 3:45 12:30 6:23 3:05 7:55 7:55 .

___ ___ ___ ___ ___ ___ ___ ___ ___
7:30 12:30 1:15 6:15 3:05 2:15 5:23 10:26 9:25

2.

___ ___ ___ ___ ___ ___ ___ ___ ___
8:15 3:45 6:15 6:23 2:15 6:23 3:05 3:45 3:10

___ ___ ___ ___ ___ ___ ___ ___ ___ ___ ___
5:23 4:05 7:55 5:23 10:26 9:25 3:05 3:45 2:55 7:55 8:15

___ ___ ___ ___ ___ ___ **?**
12:30 4:50 12:30 2:55 3:05 6:15

___ ___ ___ ___ ___ ___ ___ ___ ___ ___
3:05 7:55 3:45 12:30 7:10 3:10 12:30 6:00 7:55 7:55 6:23

___ ___ ___ ___ .
3:05 2:15 7:30 3:10

Answers on page 48

CALLING MR. PRESIDENT

You can call up some presidents of the United States by choosing the letters off the buttons of a telephone. The problem is that on a phone, each number, 2 through 9, can stand for three different letters. For example, the 2 might stand for A, B, or C. Your challenge is to decide which letter goes with each number in order to form the names of 19 American presidents.

1) 9 4 5 7 6 6

2) 7 3 2 4 2 6

3) 2 8 2 4 2 6 2 6

4) 6 4 9 6 6

5) 7 6 5 5

6) 5 4 6 2 6 5 6

7) 2 2 7 8 3 7

8) 2 3 2 6 7

9) 4 6 6 8 3 7

10) 2 8 7 4

11) 4 7 2 6 8

12) 6 2 3 4 7 6 6

13) 4 2 7 3 4 6 4

14) 8 7 8 6 2 6

15) 8 2 3 8

16) 4 2 7 3 4 3 5 3

17) 2 7 8 4 8 7

18) 5 6 4 6 7 6 6

19) 6 6 6 7 6 3

Answers on page 48

Illustrated by Terry Rogers

1 _____

2 _____

3 _____

4 _____

5 _____

6 _____

7 _____

8 _____

9 _____

10 _____

11 _____

12 _____

13 _____

14 _____

15 _____

16 _____

17 _____

18 _____

19 _____

THE DANCING MEN

Secret codes have been around a long time. The one on this page is over 100 years old. It first appeared in a Sherlock Holmes story called "The Adventure of the Dancing Men."

On the next page is a message that Dr. Watson probably never sent to Sherlock Holmes. Use the chart below to help you figure out the riddle. Letters marked with a small flag show the end of a word.

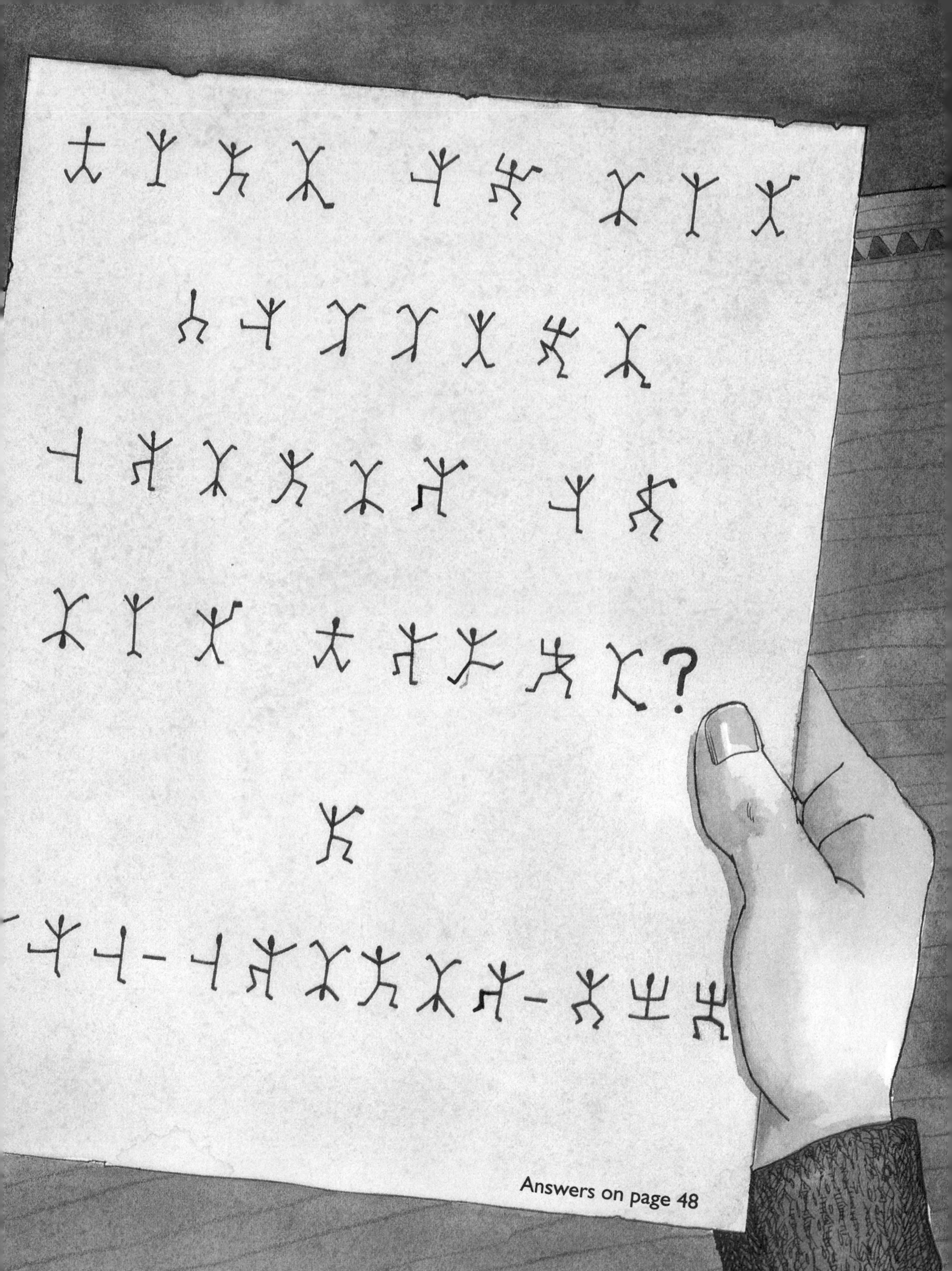

Answers on page 48

Illustrated by Anni Matsick

ANSWERS

FUN FINGERS (pages 6-7)
The deaf can converse just fine
By using a language that's signed.
They don't need to shout
To get their words out
Or to send you this message
  in rhyme.

DOTS ALL (pages 8-9)
What are the three quickest ways of spreading a secret? **Telephone, telegraph, and tell your little sister.**

FLAG FUN (pages 10-11)
A BOAT
CARRYING A
SHIPMENT OF
YO-YOS ACROSS
THE OCEAN
SPRANG A LEAK
AND SANK
FIFTY TIMES

A TOUCHY LANGUAGE (pages 12-13)
This language was invented by a student in France. The dots are pressed into paper to come out as tiny bumps that allow blind people to read by feeling the letters with their fingers. The language is called Braille.

BOAT CODE (pages 14-15)
1. **Mayflower**   6. **Bounty**
2. **Constitution** 7. **Monitor**
3. **Nina**   8. **Titanic**
4. **Maine**   9. **Half Moon**
5. **Pinta**   10. **Santa Maria**

TRAFFIC STOPPERS (pages 16-17)
A clean car is a happy car!
A dirty car is a grime!
Grime does not pay!

GOAT TELL YOUR MOTHER (pages 18-19)
He's my kid brother.

ROUNDABOUT RIDDLE (pages 20-21)
Because it's the "scenter."

THE ROYAL FAMILY (page 22)
Queen Gwendolyn   King Kesworth
Prince Wally   Lord Larry
Princess Pearl   Baron Barracuda
Duchess Teresa   Countess Sarah

DOTS A LOT (page 23)
What two inventions help people get up in the world? **Elevators and Alarm Clocks**

A CRYPTIC CRYPT (pages 24-25)
Why couldn't the mummy go to the Monster Mash party? **He was too wrapped up in his work.**

How does a mummy get help in a good hotel? **He calls "tomb" service.**

A CLEAN CODE (pages 26-27)
What do you call it when pigs do their laundry? **Hogwash.**

Where do sheep get their hair cut? **At the baa-baa shop.**

ICE-CREAM CODES (pages 28-29)
How do you learn to work in an ice-cream parlor? **You go to Sundae School.**

MUSICAL MERRIMENT (pages 30-31)
What do musical ghosts need before they play their instruments? **Sheet music.**

THE MYSTERY OF THE CASTLE (pages 32-33)
My business is building castles of stone, for kings, for queens, and for storing the throne.

My fun comes from hiding these words in the walls, in a code that is carved in one of the halls.

TAKE THE FIELD (pages 34-35)
Why is it farther from second base to third than it is from first base to second? **Because there's a shortstop in between.**

RIDING THE RAILS (pages 36-37)

1	2	3	4	5	6	7	8	9	10	11	12	13	14	15
11	22	100	22	3	13	7	21	100	3	100	14	17	22	100
I	T		T	A	K	E	S		A		L	O	T	

16	17	18	19	20	21	22	23	24	25	26	27	28	29	30
17	8	100	21	22	7	3	15	100	3	16	6	100	3	100
O	F		S	T	E	A	M		A	N	D		A	

31	32	33	34	35	36	37	38	39	40	41	42	43	44	45
17	16	7	0	22	20	3	5	13	100	15	11	16	6	2
O	N	E	-	T	R	A	C	K		M	I	N	D	.

LOOK OUT BELOW! (pages 38-39)
S Q U I D N A P P E R S
1 2 3 4 5 6 7 8 8 9 10 1

CORNY CODE (pages 40-41)
What kind of fruit do scarecrows like? **Strawberries**

Why are cornstalks good listeners? **Because they're all ears**

HARD TIMES (pages 42-43)
Why did the clock get a rash? **It had too many ticks.**

Why did the clocks throw a party? **To have a good time.**

CALLING MR. PRESIDENT (pages 44-45)
1) **Wilson**   11) **Grant**
2) **Reagan**   12) **Madison**
3) **Buchanan**   13) **Harding**
4) **Nixon**   14) **Truman**
5) **Polk**   15) **Taft**
6) **Lincoln**   16) **Garfield**
7) **Carter**   17) **Arthur**
8) **Adams**   18) **Johnson**
9) **Hoover**   19) **Monroe**
10) **Bush**

THE DANCING MEN (pages 46-47)
What is the biggest potato in the world? **A hip-potato-mus.**